The Witches' Marriage

2

studio HEADLINE

CONTENTS

The Witch's Fortune-Telling

THAT TIME...
I NEED YOU, TANYA.
I DON'T WANT ANYONE ELSE.
SO DON'T GO.
...IS WHAT I SAID.
KAAA (BLUSH)
I'M SO EMBAR-RASSED!!

WHAT'S WRONG, MELISSA?
HA (GASP)
KIRA (SPARKLE)
KIRA
...
IT'S NOTHING! SEE YOU LATER!
WHA—!? SO FAST!
BYUN (ZOOM)
IT'S NOT NOTHING.
EVER SINCE WE FINISHED THE TRIAL ...
...I HAVEN'T BEEN ABLE TO LOOK TANYA IN THE EYE!
YOUNG LADY.

IF YOU PUT ON AIRS, SHE'LL BREAK UP WITH YOU.
WHAT?
SO MANY WITCHES ARE TERRIBLY PRIDEFUL, YOU KNOW?
I'VE SEEN GIRLS LIKE YOU GET DUMPED MANY TIMES.
HAAH... DEAR ME.
ACCORDING TO MY PARTNER READING, YOU TWO ARE...
SHA
READ-ING!?
SHA (SWISH)
HEY!
I DIDN'T ASK YOU TO TELL MY FORTUNE!
BA (FWIP)

OH MY!
IT'S THE SHEARS OF SEPARATION.
A CARD OF GREAT MISFORTUNE THAT SELDOM APPEARS.
THE LAST TIME I SAW IT WAS PERHAPS A HUNDRED YEARS AGO.
THE SHEARS ...
I KNOW THIS CARD...
YORO (SHAKE)
IF THE BLADES POINT DOWNWARD WHEN THIS CARD IS DRAWN, IT MEANS YOUR TIES WILL BE CUT.
BY THE TIME YOU SEE IT, IT IS TOO LATE TO DO ANYTHING ...
...FOR YOUR RELATIONSHIP WITH YOUR PARTNER...!!

HOW COULD I PULL SUCH A TERRIBLE CARD...!?
YOU RECENT-LY...
...TOLD YOUR PARTNER A TRUTH YOU HAD BEEN HIDING, DIDN'T YOU?
BUT UNTIL THEN...
...YOU LOOKED DOWN ON HER AND DECEIVED HER.
AFTER SUCH BEHAVIOR ...
...DON'T YOU THINK IT'S TOO LATE...
...TO POUR YOUR HEART OUT NOW?
WHAT'S UP? GOT YOUR FORTUNE TOLD?
HYOKO (POP)

TANYA!
WHAT'S THIS CARD?
THIS CARD IS ALMOST NEVER DRAWN.
IT IS CALLED THE SHEARS OF SEPA-RATION.
SO BASI-CALLY... THAT MEANS...
...IT'S A RARE CARD!
WOOOw!
WHAT ARE YOU SO HAPPY ABOUT?
WHEN THE BLADES ON THIS CARD POINT DOWN-WARD—
HA (GASP)

THE BLADES ARE FACING UPWARD NOW...
WHAT A PUSHY GIRL!
KYA-HA-HA!
BUT NOT IN A BAD WAY.
WHEN THE BLADES POINT UPWARD, IT MEANS YOU HAVE A STRONG, UTTERLY UNBREAKABLE BOND!
IS THAT TRUE?
THAT SOUNDS JUST LIKE US!
......
HEE HEE.
MELISSA?

YOU'RE TOO MUCH...!
AS LONG AS I'M WITH TANYA...
...EVERYTHING WILL BE ALL RIGHT.
HUH? WHERE'S THE FORTUNE-TELLER LADY?
HEH HEH ...
I THINK THOSE TWO...
...ARE GOING TO BE INTER-ESTING.

DELIVERY! DELIVERY HERE!
BASA (FLAP)
BASA
THANK YOU, MR. FAMILIAR!
DOKI (BADUM)
DOKI
Thank you for your order.
The Witch's Kiss
If you pour magic into this Witch's Rose and let it bloom, believe it or not, your power will increase.
...I BOUGHT THIS WITHOUT TELLING MELISSA.
I'M GOING TO POWER UP MY MAGIC AND SURPRISE HER!
However...
AH!
CHIKU (PRICK)
...watch out for the thorns.
TANYA, WHAT DID YOU GET FROM THAT SHOP...?

!?
WHAT'S WRONG?
MY CHEST IS BURNING ...
THIS IS...
It's the curse of the Witch's Rose.
I told her to be careful.
I'M SORRY...
Relax. There is a way to break the curse.
QUIT BEING DRAMATIC. SPIT IT OUT!
You seem awfully desperate, hmm?
NIYA (GRIN)
NIYA
SH- SHE'S MY PARTNER. I CAN'T HELP IT.

The curse will continue to sap its bearer's power until she dies.
There is only one way to lift it—
A kiss from her partner.
!?
Pour magic directly into the mark from your lips.
CHUUU (MWAH)
THAT'S RIDICU-LOUS!!
KURU (TURN)
I CAN'T DEAL WITH THIS.

ORO ORO (FRET)
M-MELISSA...
A KISS WITH TANYA?
HMPH!
I CAN'T PICTURE IT!
MELISSA!
I LOVE YOU!
MELISSA!
THANKS TO YOU, MELISSA!
I MEAN...
I'VE NEVER KISSED ANYONE BEFORE!
DOKI (BADUM)
DOKI
UM...
THERE MUST BE SOME OTHER WAY...
SOWA SOWA (FIDGET)
I'LL BE FINE.
SEE? I'M ALL BET—
DOKUN (THUMP)

TANYA!?
HAA (PANT)
HAA
ZUZUZU (CREEP)
THE MARK IS SAPPING TANYA'S MAGIC.
IT'S ALL RIGHT, MELISSA.
THIS IS MY PUNISHMENT.
HAA
HAA
I DON'T HAVE MUCH POWER, BUT I WANTED TO PUSH MYSELF...
...AND GET A LITTLE BIT CLOSER TO YOU...

SO THIS...
GAKU (SLUMP)
SHE PASSED OUT.
TANYA!!
OPEN YOUR EYES!
HAA (PANT)
HAA
I WANTED TO PUSH MYSELF ...
...MY DREAM IS...
AT THIS RATE, NO MATTER HOW LONG I TRY, I'LL NEVER BE LIKE MELISSA...
IS THE ONE WITCH IN THE WORLD
...TO BECOME A WITCH LIKE YOU, MELISSA.
...WHO'S MOST ABLE TO ACHIEVE HER OWN DREAMS.
...AND GET A LITTLE BIT CLOSER TO YOU...
GYU (SQUEEZE)
...YOU REALLY ARE...
...A SILLY GIRL.

HUH...?
IT DOESN'T HURT.
MUKU (RISE)
I'M HEALED? HOW...?
KAAA (BLUSH)
......
MELISSA, DID YOU ......?
YEAH? SO WHAT IF I DID!?
CHIKU (PRICK)
OH NO! THIS TIME, IT'S MY TURN!
!??! ???

The Witch's Growth
LAST TIME, TANYA FELL UNDER THE CURSE OF THE WITCH'S ROSE...
...BUT WITH MELISSA'S HELP, THE CRISIS PASSED.
...OR SO IT SEEMED.
EEK!
BAN (BAM)
TANYA, WHAT'S WRONG !?
!?
I...
...GOT BIGGER?

It's a side effect of the curse of the Witch's Rose.
It appears that the young miss's innate magical power has run wild.
No need to worry. She'll return to normal after a little while.
BYE NOW!
OF ALL THE ANNOY-ING—
LET'S JUST HAVE SOME TEA AND RELAX.
THIS IS ALL YOUR FAULT, YOU KNOW!
GACHAN (CLATTER)
AH!

....
WHAT ARE YOU DOING?
GU (CLENCH)
KATSUN (CLINK)
WHOA! COOL!
I WISHED FOR IT TO GO BACK TO NORMAL, AND OUT CAME MAGIC!
THAT WAS...

...A TIME REVERSAL SPELL.
AN ADVANCED SPELL THAT TURNS BACK TIME.
HOW DID TANYA MANAGE THAT!?
EVEN I CAN'T PULL IT OFF!
LOOK, MELISSA!
S-SO? ANYONE COULD DO A LITTLE THING LIKE THAT!
O...OH, RIGHT.
I BET THIS WOULD BE EASY FOR YOU!
GAH!
ピュアアアアッ
PYUAAAA (PURE)

REGARD-LESS, THIS MAGIC...
...IS THE FULLY GROWN TANYA'S...
...NATURAL POWER.
I WORKED HARD TO GET TO WHERE I AM TODAY...
...BUT THIS GIRL CAN DO AN ADVANCED SPELL JUST LIKE THAT...
!?

POTO (DRIP)
WH- WHAT'S WRONG!?
AH HA HA!
I'M JUST KINDA RELIEVED...
THROUGH A WITCHES' MARRIAGE, YOU'RE SUPPOSED TO BECOME AN AMAZING WITCH, BUT...
...I'M ALWAYS COMPLETELY USELESS.
SO I'M GLAD TO KNOW IT TURNS OUT...
...THAT I'LL BE A BIT BETTER WHEN I GROW UP.
GYU (GRIP)

I WAS ALWAYS WORRIED ABOUT...
...WHETHER I'D BE ANY HELP TO YOU.

WHAT ARE YOU TALKING ABOUT?

MELISSA
...

YOU'VE WORKED HARD THIS WHOLE TIME.

IT GOES WITHOUT SAYING THAT YOU'RE CAPABLE.

GYU (HUG)

WA—

...SHE'S IMPOSSIBLE.

THE SIDE EFFECTS CLEARED UP AFTER A GOOD NIGHT'S SLEEP.

I FEEL BETTER!

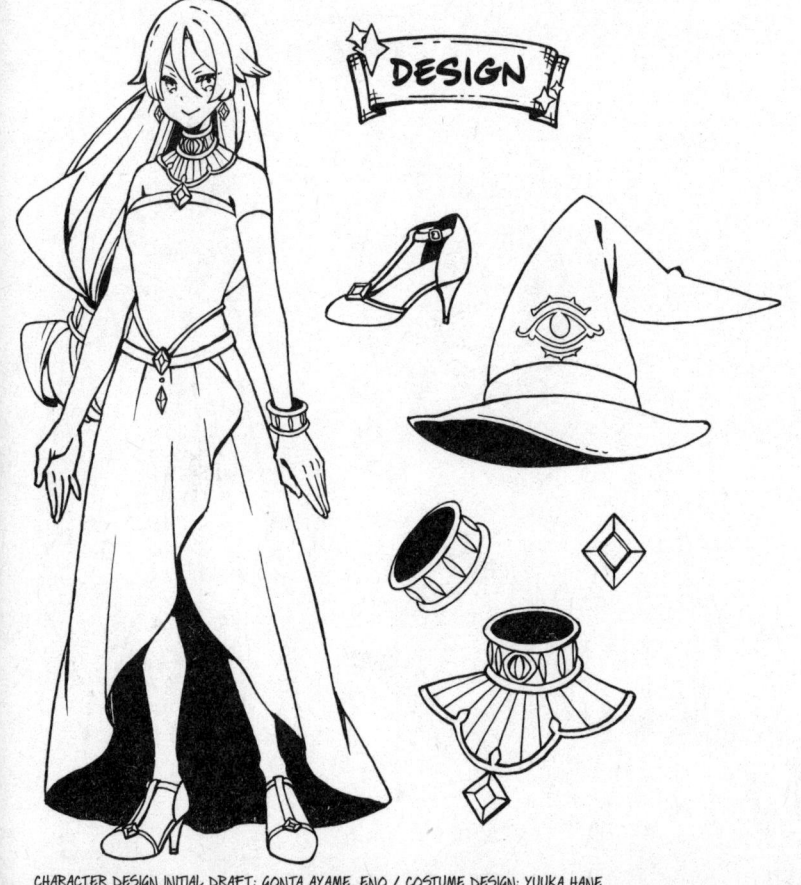

CHARACTER DESIGN INITIAL DRAFT: GONTA AYAME, ENO / COSTUME DESIGN: YUUKA HANE

DESIGN

CHARACTER DESIGN INITIAL DRAFT: YUUSHI HASHIMOTO / COSTUME DESIGN: YUUKA HANE

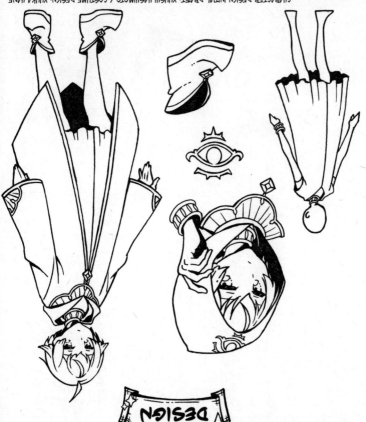

The Witch's True Thoughts

TANYA, I BOUGHT SOME CANDY, WANT ONE?

REALLY?

THANK YOOOU!

PAKU (CHOMP)

MMM!

THE SWEETNESS OF FRUIT AND THE FRESH TASTE OF MINT SPREADING THROUGH MY MOUTH...

HOWAWAAAN (GLOW)

THIS IS...

TOTALLY DISGUST-ING.
テッテレ～
TETTEREEE (HOORAY)
I'M GONNA THROW UP!
HUH? THAT'S NOT WHAT I...
WHAT!?
...FOR NOW, THE EXPERIMENT IS A SUCCESS.
AN INVERSION SPELL, WORD REVERSE.
!?
A SPELL THAT MAKES PEOPLE SAY THE OPPOSITE OF WHAT THEY INTEND.
YES
NO

I WANTED TO TEST IF I COULD ADD THAT SPELL INTO THE CANDY.
WOW!
TO MAKE SOMETHING LIKE THAT...
YOU MUST REALLY HAVE NO LIFE.
GUSA (STAB)
OH-NO!
I—I MEAN...!
...I KNOW.
IT'S NOT WHAT YOU REALLY THINK.
UHH... UHH...
NO!
YOU'RE SO MEAN —
MEDIO-CRE...
LAZY...

I UNDERSTAND, BUT...

...IT'S GETTING ANNOYING.

I JUST HAVE TO THINK OF THE OPPOSITE WORDS!

イライラ IRA
イライラ IRA (IRK)

HA (GASP)

I'VE GOT IT!

......

THE OPPO- SITE...

IF I INSULT YOU...

PORO
PORO (DRIP)
!?
WAAH W—
...
EVEN IF I'D BE LYING...
HIKU (HIC)
...THE IDEA OF INSULTING YOU...
...IS SO...
GYO (SHOCK)

I HAVE TO DO SOMETHING...

...BUT GIVING GENTLE REASSURANCE IS EMBARRASSING. I CAN'T!

I WENT TOO FAR...

HA (GASP)

HIKKU (HIC)

I'M MAKING MELISSA FEEL AWKWARD AGAIN...

HIKKU

..TANYA.

THANK YOU. I DIDN'T GO TOO FAR.
THE INSULTS REALLY BOTHER ME, SO...
... DON'T FORGIVE ME.
?
?
WHAT'S MELISSA SAYING?
?
MOGO (MUNCH)
MOGO
!
MOGO
AH!
THEN THAT WAS...

I'M SORRY. I WENT TOO FAR
THE INSULTS DON'T BOTHER ME AT ALL, SO...
...FORGIVE ME?
I'LL NEVER FORGIVE YOU! (YOU DIDN'T BOTHER ME EITHER!)
!?
THINGS WERE CONFUSING, SO THE TWO OF THEM DIDN'T TALK FOR A WHILE.

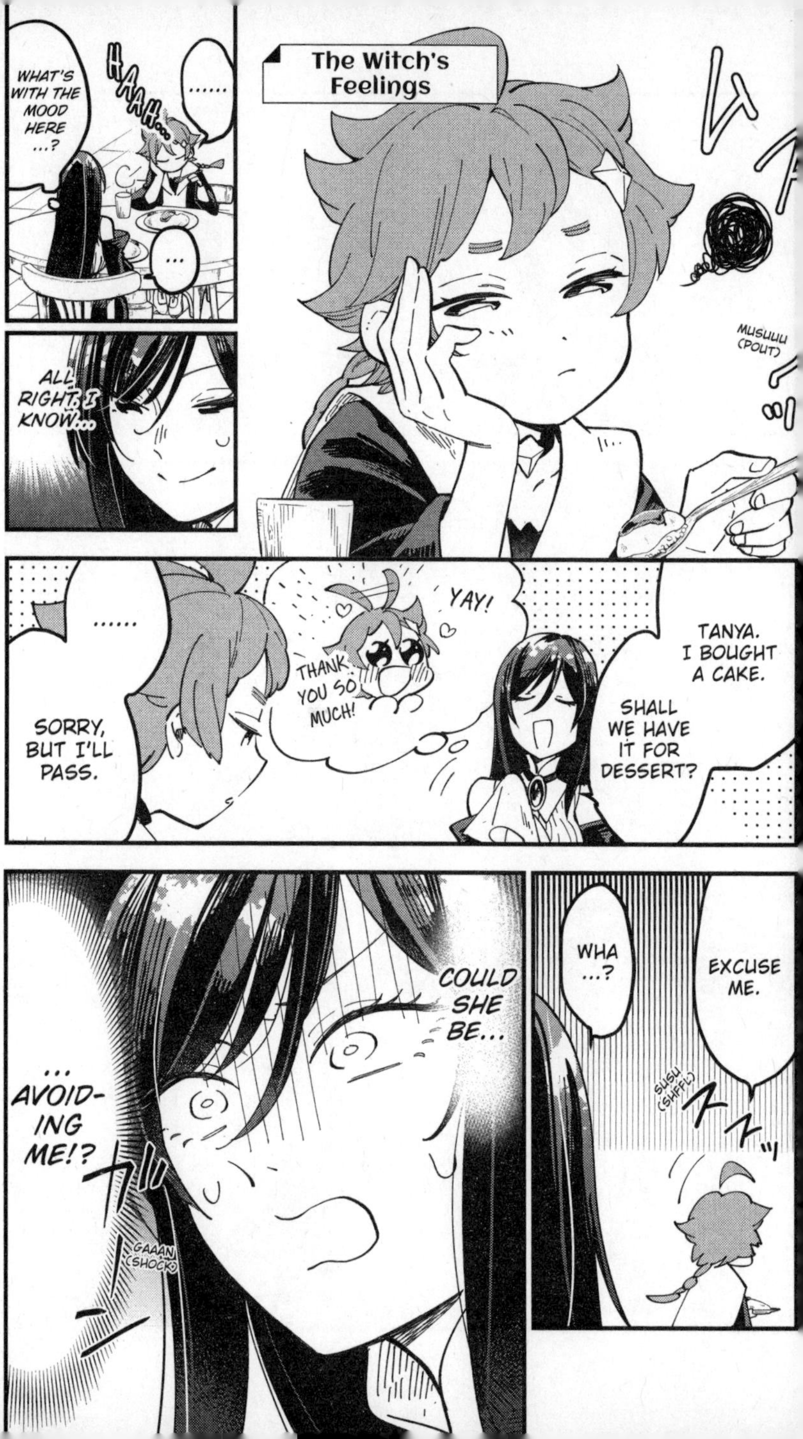
The Witch's Feelings
Musuuu (POUT)
WHAT'S WITH THE MOOD HERE ...?
HAAAH...
......
...
ALL RIGHT, I KNOW...
TANYA. I BOUGHT A CAKE.
SHALL WE HAVE IT FOR DESSERT?
YAY!
THANK YOU SO MUCH!
......
SORRY, BUT I'LL PASS.
EXCUSE ME.
WHA ...?
Susu (SHFFL)
COULD SHE BE...
... AVOID-ING ME!?
GAAAN (SHOCK)

AS IF!
TANYA WOULD NEVER...
....
DON'T TELL ME...
...SHE'S STILL ANGRY AT ME FOR USING HER AS A GUINEA PIG THE OTHER DAY?
BUT I APOL-OGIZED FOR THAT (USING THE OPPOSITE WORDS).
IT'S OVER AND DONE WITH.
......

TANYA!

......

WHAT IS IT?

I WANT TO TALK TO YOU...

?

プル
PURU

プルル
PURU
(TREMBLE)

I CAN'T PUT IT INTO WORDS.

WHAT DO I DO?

39

TANYA ALWAYS UNDER-STANDS ME.
WHY NOT TODAY...?
......
CAN I GO NOW?
!?
WAIT!
AT TIMES LIKE THIS, MY MISTRESS WOULD SAY...
SHION WAS CRYING, YOU KNOW.

ISN'T THERE SOMETHING YOU SHOULD TELL HER AT A TIME LIKE THIS?

...... LISTEN...

... MELISSA ...

...IF YOU DON'T SAY ANYTHING, OTHER PEOPLE WON'T KNOW HOW YOU FEEL.

TANYA.

SO FACE HER PROPERLY.

I'M SORRY ABOUT THE OTHER DAY!

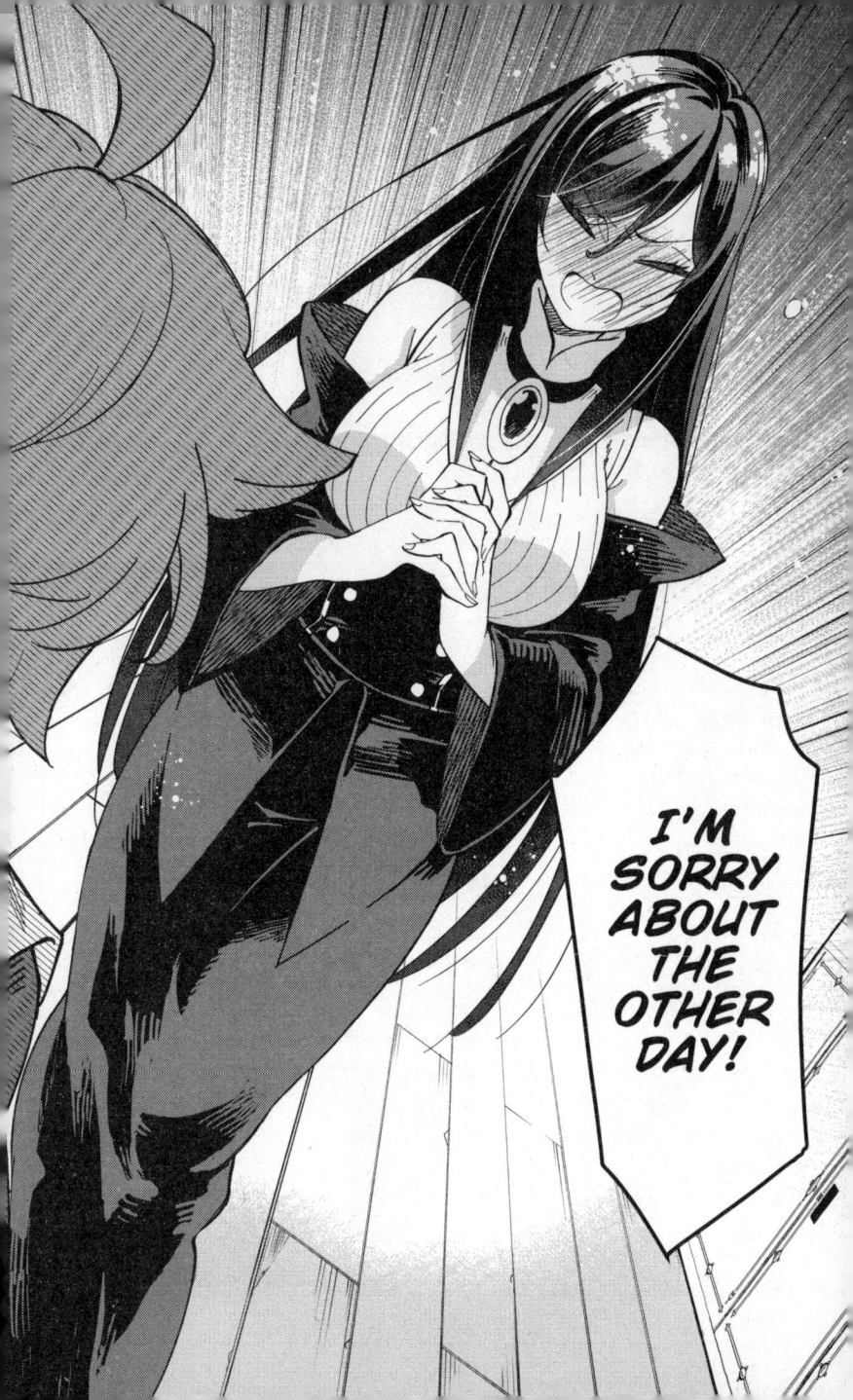

SHIIIN (SILENCE)
BUT YOU'VE LOOKED ANGRY ALL DAY...
WHAT DO YOU MEAN?
HUH !?
THAT'S 'COS ...
...MY TOOTH HAS BEEN HURTING SINCE THIS MORNING.
THAT'S WHY I COULDN'T EAT MY FOOD OR THE CAKE.
WHAAAAT!?
WEREN'T YOU AVOIDING ME!?
AVOIDING YOU?
NO WAY!

I COULD NEVER HATE YOU, MELISSA.
NIPAA (SMILE)
KYUN (THROB)
.........!
YOU'RE SO CON-FUSING!
???
... GOOD GRIEF.
COME IN. I'LL GIVE YOU MEDICINE FOR THE PAIN.
OKAY!
SFX: GYUUU (SQUEEZE)

ZAA (FSSHH)
ZAA
The Witches' Game
RAINY DAYS ARE SO BORING.
HAAAH...
I'VE GOT IT!
THIS CALLS FOR...
?
GOSO GOSO (RUMMAGE)

...OLD WITCH! WANNA PLAY?

OLD WITCH?

IT'S A GAME THAT WAS POPULAR WHERE I'M FROM.

JAAAN
(TA-DAAA)

KURUN
(TURN)

USE THIS TIME TO STUDY.

!!

NO.

......

SHUN
(SUU)

...RIGHT.

...JUST ONE ROUND.
BOSO (MUTTER)
I'LL JOIN YOU FOR JUST ONE ROUND.
!
GOKU (GULP)
BA (GRAB)
DEDEEEN (WOMP-WOMP)
WH-WHY DON'T WE PLAY ONE MORE TIME?

ニャァッ
NIYAA
(SMIRK)

ぐっ
GU
(CLENCH)

ずーん
ZUUUN
(GLOOM)

MELISSA IS EASY TO READ.

AH!

ひょい
HYOI
(LIFT)

HOW CAN I LOSE!?

IT'S TANYA, OF ALL PEOPLE...

COME ON!

ONE MORE ROUND!
BAN (BAM)
ONE MORE ROUND!
DEN (WHAM)
DON (WHUMP)
ONE MORE ROUND!
AGAIN! ONE MORE ROUND!!
MUKIII (ROAR)
O- OKAY.
MELISSA ...
...SURE IS GETTING HEATED.

GUI (PUSH)
ゲイ

7♥

......

GIKU (JOLT)
ギク

ARE YOU TRYING TO HELP ME?

GUI
グイ

......

GUI
グイ

GUI
グイ

SHAAA (SWISH)
ニャーッ

...DO YOU THINK I WOULD BE PLEASED WITH A PITY WIN?

I—

TANYA...

THERE'S NO NEED TO HOLD BACK IN COMPE-TITION!
COME AT ME WITH EVERYTHING YOU'VE GOT!
GOT IT!
NEXT TIME, I WON'T GO EASY ON YOU.
THAT'S RIGHT.
MELISSA IS...

...STUBBORN, COMPETITIVE...
...AND NEVER GIVES UP, EVEN IF SHE FAILS.
THOSE ASPECTS OF HER ARE TRULY...
YOU LOSE AGAIN, MELISSA.
WHAT!? ONE MORE!!

PICNIC DAY! PICNIC DAY!
LET'S MAKE TASTY SANDWICHES! ♪
The Witch's Support
PURU (TREMBLE) PURU PURU
GUNUNU (GRR)
WHEN HOLDING A KITCHEN KNIFE, REMEMBER THE KITTY PAW! ♪
MEOW!
I—I KNOW, IT'S JUST... HARD...TO CONTROL...
I'M KIND OF BAD AT COOKING— OKAY, REALLY BAD— BUT...
DOROOO (OOZE)
...I DON'T WANT TO DISGRACE MYSELF IN FRONT OF HER!
FINISHED!

GUCHAAA (MESSY)
IT TASTES GOOD, THOUGH.
URK...
SFX: PAKU (CHOMP)
THERE'S JUST A FEW TOO MANY INGREDI- ENTS.
IF WE ADJUST THE AMOUNT...
...SEE? IT LOOKS DELICIOUS.
HMPH.
YOU DON'T HAVE TO TELL ME THAT! I CAN FIGURE IT OUT MYSELF!
PA (PUFF)
PA
BUWAAA (KABOOM)

TEKIPAKI (BRISK)
WHY?
I FOLLOW THE RECIPES CORRECTLY...
...BUT NO MATTER HOW MANY TIMES I TRY, I CAN'T MAKE ANYTHING PERFECT.
WHY IS TANYA SO MUCH BETTER THAN ME!?
KYAA
I DON'T UNDERSTAND IT...
HURRY UP, MELISSA!
! THAT BROOM-STICK ...
IT'S MINE.

I THINK MY POWER'S JUST ABOUT GROWN ENOUGH ...
...FOR ME TO RIDE A BROOM TOO.
ALL RIGHT!
GU (CLENCH)
LET'S GOOO !!
FUWA (FWOOSH)
!?
BATAAAN (THUD)
ACK!!
OUCH...

HEH...

YOU MAY BE GREAT AROUND THE HOUSE, BUT...

WHAT'S THIS?

HA (GASP)

...YOUR MAGIC STILL NEEDS SOME WORK.

...DID I JUST...
GYU (CLENCH)
...SEE TANYA FAIL TO USE MAGIC...
...AND FEEL RELIEVED?
I GUESS I STILL CAN'T DO IT AFTER ALL...
...I'M THE WORST.

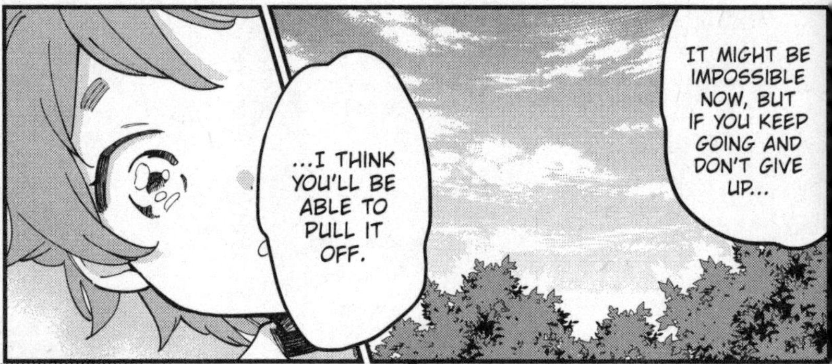
IT MIGHT BE IMPOSSIBLE NOW, BUT IF YOU KEEP GOING AND DON'T GIVE UP...
...I THINK YOU'LL BE ABLE TO PULL IT OFF.

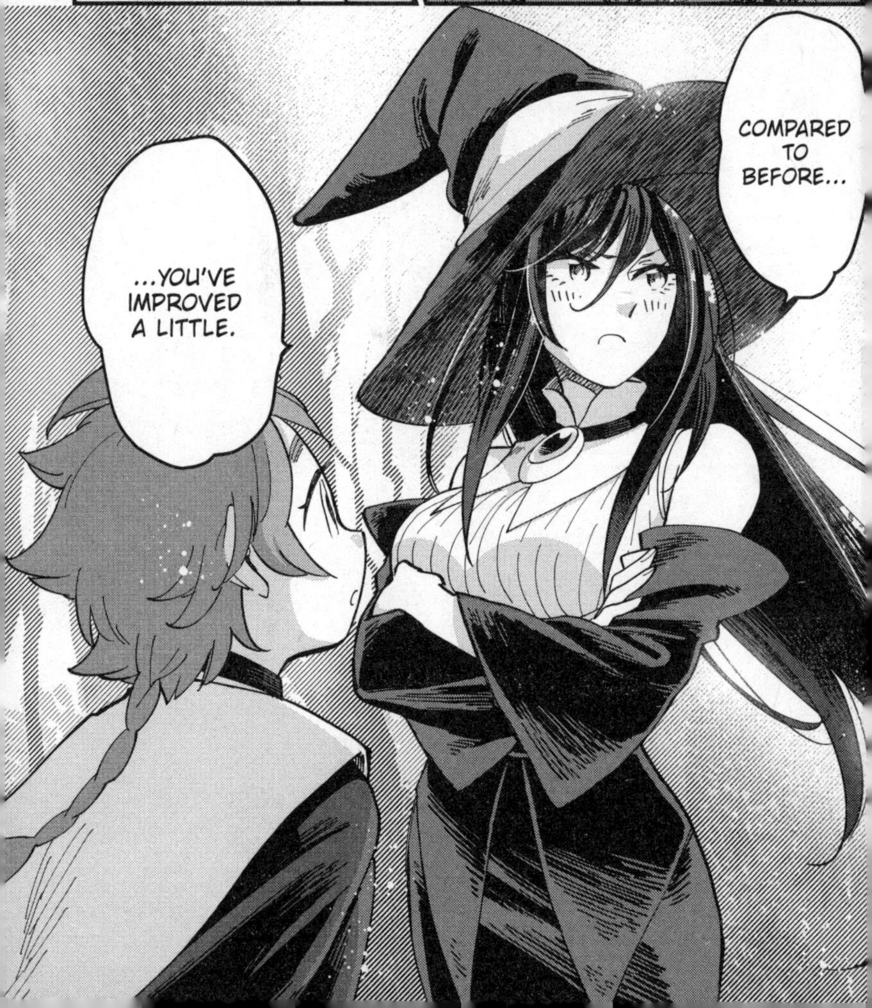
COMPARED TO BEFORE...
...YOU'VE IMPROVED A LITTLE.

...THE SAME GOES FOR MY COOKING, RIGHT?
MELISSA ...
COME ON. LET'S GET GOING.
OKAY!

DESIGN

CHARACTER DESIGN: HINATA MIKAGE

DESIGN

CHARACTER DESIGN INITIAL DRAFT: SHINO SHIMIZU, GONTA AYAME / COSTUME DESIGN: YUUKA HANE

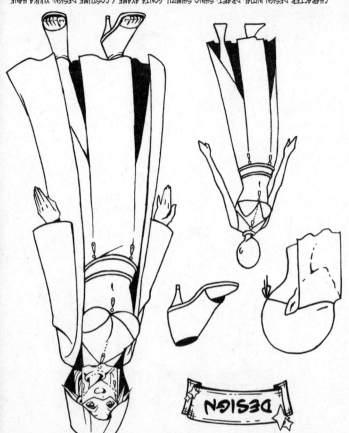

WHOOO!!
FLYING ON A BROOMSTICK FEELS SO NICE!
The Witches' School
SETTLE DOWN. I CAN'T CONCENTRATE.
THERE IT IS.
THE WITCHES' MARRIAGE COLLEGE— WMC.
A FEW WEEKS EARLIER
IT'S HERE!
OUR WMC ADMISSION LETTER!
PAAA (GLOW)

IS THAT IMPRES- SIVE?
OF COURSE.
ENROLLING IN WMC IS ONE OF THE MILESTONES OF A WITCHES' MARRIAGE...
...AND WE'VE BEEN ACCEPTED!
THE WITCHES' MARRIAGE COLLEGE, ALSO KNOWN AS WMC.
A SCHOOL WHERE COUPLES WHO ARE IN A WITCHES' MARRIAGE TRAIN SO THEY CAN OPEN THE DOORS OF TRUTH.
IT OFFERS VARIOUS CLASSES TO DEEPEN BONDS AND INCREASE MAGICAL POWER. ONLY A CHOSEN FEW ARE ABLE TO ATTEND.
I'M ONE STEP CLOSER TO THE DOORS OF TRUTH...AND TO MY MISTRESS!
SO...
...IF WE GO TO THIS SCHOOL ...
...MY POWER WILL INCREASE TOO!?
LET'S HEAD THERE RIGHT AWAY!

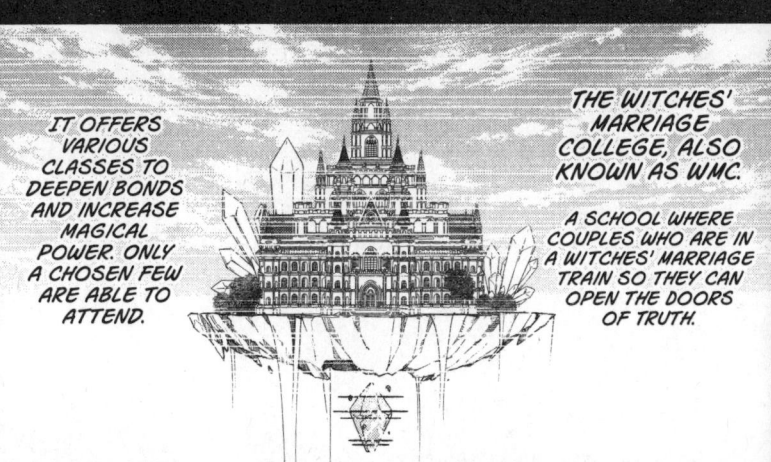

SO THIS IS A WITCHES' CLASS-ROOM.
IT LOOKS KINDA FUN!
WAI (CHAT-TER)
WAI
THERE ARE ALL KINDS OF PEOPLE HERE.
ANY SPECIES IS ALLOWED— YOU JUST HAVE TO BE A WITCH.
I'M GONNA GO LOOK OVER THERE!
TATATA (DASH)
WAIT!
WAH!
DON (WHAM)
I'M SO SORRY!
IT'S OKAY ...

OH.
IF IT ISN'T MELIS-SA.
I'M AMAZED YOU'RE HERE, SEEING AS YOU DON'T KEEP PARTNERS FOR VERY LONG.
GO (RUMBLE)
GO
GO
GO
SAME TO YOU, SHION.
PLAYING WITH DOLLS IN A PLACE LIKE THIS?
HMPH! NOTHING YOU SAY WILL HURT ME.
THIS TIME, VICTORY IS MINE.
WHY...?

'COS OF YOU!
BISHI (POINT)
YOU CAN'T RIDE A BROOMSTICK BY YOURSELF.
FOR A WITCH, FLYING ON A BROOM IS THE MOST BASIC OF ALL BASICS!
IF YOU'RE NOT EVEN CAPABLE OF THAT...
...YOU'LL JUST GET IN YOUR PARTNER'S WAY.
SO COME BACK WHEN YOU'VE FIGURED IT OUT!
HO HO HO!
SAYS THE ONE WHO USED TO RUN AFTER ME IN TEARS WHEN SHE COULDN'T USE FLYING MAGIC.
WAIT, MELISSA!
TH-THAT WAS WHEN I WAS A CHILD!!

I HATE IT WHEN YOU DO THAT!
STUPID, STUPID MELISSA!
SHUTATATA (DASH)
DÉJÀ VU...
FORGET HER. LET'S TAKE A SEAT.
......
KURU (TURN)
GUI (GRAB)

69

THE FOR-TUNE-TELLER LADY!

MY NAME IS BARBARA.

NICE TO MEET YOU!

WELCOME TO WMC!

COUPLES WHO FAIL...

I KNOW WE JUST STARTED, BUT LET'S HAVE A TEST.

!?

...WILL BE EXPELLED IMMEDIATELY!

GOOD LUCK! ♥

THE GOAL OF THIS TEST IS...
...TO FIGURE OUT WHICH IS YOUR PARTNER!
THE IMPOSTORS ARE MY FAMILIARS.
IF YOU HAVE A BOND, SURELY YOU CAN TELL THEM APART!
I'M THE REAL ONE!
IT'S ME!
IF THAT'S ALL...
GYU (GRAB)
THIS IS THE REAL ONE!
EEK!?
PON (POP)
TOO BAD! YOU FAIL, SO YOU'RE OUT!

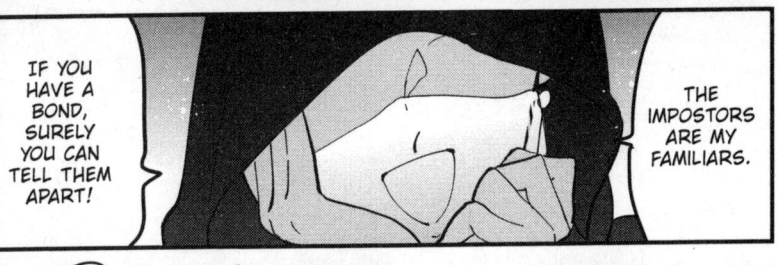

HOW COULD YOU GET THAT WRONG !?
GYAI
IT'S NOT MY FAULT!!
GYAI (SCREAM)
OH DEAR.
AND THEY WERE GETTING ALONG SO WELL BEFORE. ♪
WAAA (ROAR)
WAAA
THIS IS EASY.
DON (BAM)
SHION.
IF YOU HAVE A DEEP BOND LIKE US—
SHE LOOKED AT MY JOINTS AND COULD TELL THAT I WAS A GOLEM.
DON'T GIVE IT AWAY, LEHM!

THAT'S ALL WELL AND GOOD... IF YOUR PARTNER IS A GOLEM.
I'M THE REAL ONE!
NO, I AM!
THEIR VOICES AND GESTURES MATCH PERFECTLY!
BE QUIET SO I CAN CHOOSE!
BIKU (JOLT)
OKAY.
......
THIS TH— ONE...
ARE YOU SURE?

IS THAT REALLY HER?
IF YOU'RE WRONG ...
... LITTLE TANYA ...
...WILL BE TERRIBLY SAD.
WHICH ONE? WHICH ONE OF THEM...
...IS THE REAL TANYA!?
HA! (GASP)

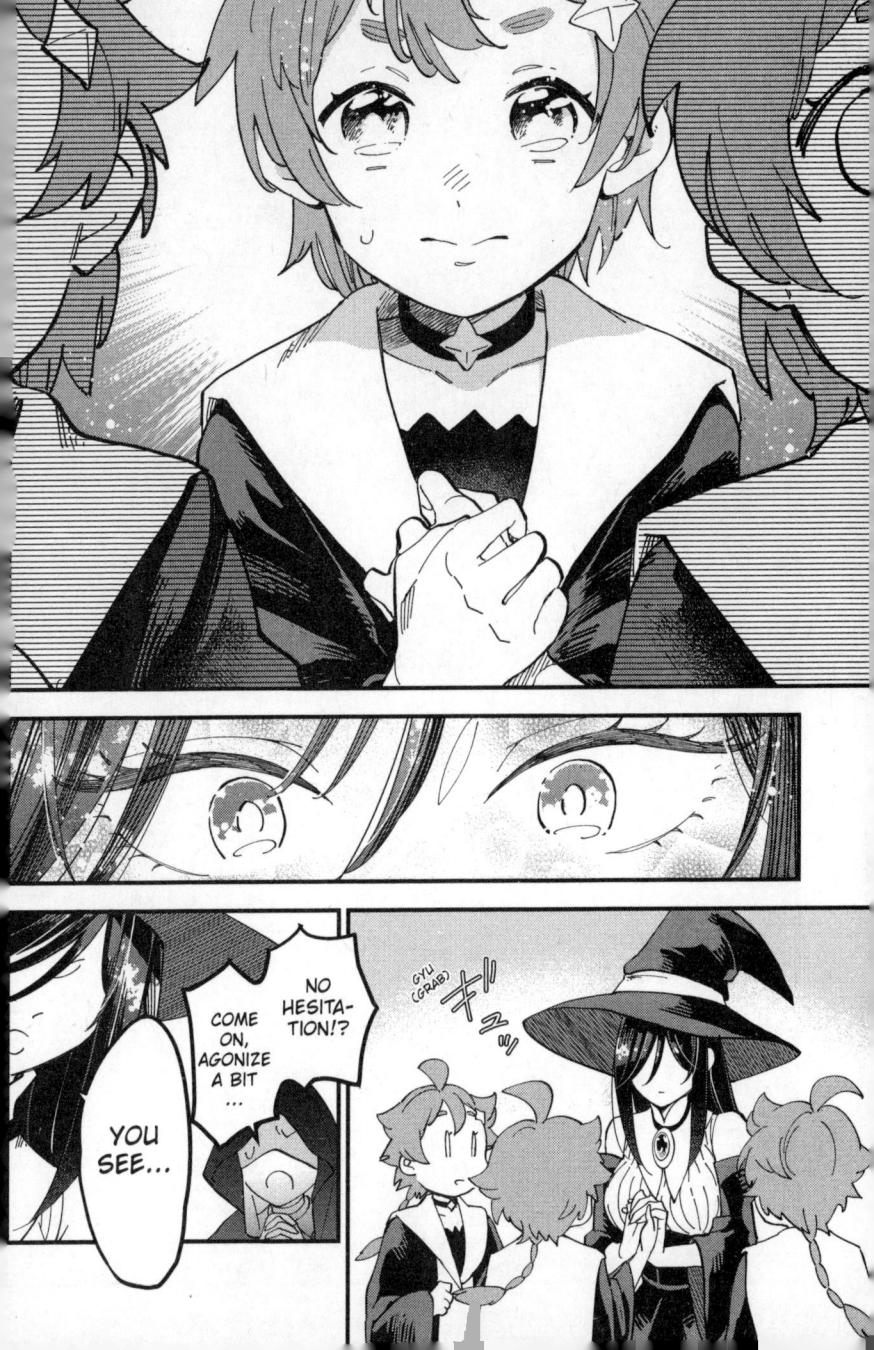

GYU (GRAB)
NO HESITATION!?
COME ON, AGONIZE A BIT ...
YOU SEE...

...TANYA ALWAYS BELIEVES IN ME, NO MATTER THE SITUATION...
...AND I CAN SEE THAT IN HER EYES!
MELISSA!

PON (POP)
CONGRAT-ULATIONS! YOU PASS!
I ACTUALLY WANTED YOU TO STRUGGLE A LITTLE MORE, THOUGH.
THIS WOMAN ...
I KNEW MY JUDGMENT WAS IMPECCABLE.
THEY ARE INEXPERIENCED, BUT THEY HAVE A STRONG SPARK.
WILL THEY BE ABLE TO MAKE USE OF THAT SPARK...?
HEH-HEH... HOW EXCITING.

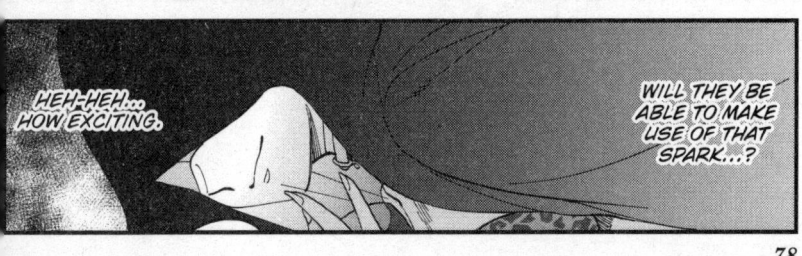

WELL DONE TO EVERYON WHO PASSED ♡
THE NEXT CLASS IS IN A WEEK'S TIME.
SEE YOU THEN!
KURU (TURN)
I CAN'T WAIT FOR NEXT WEEK! HOW ABOUT YOU, MELISSA?
The Witch's Declaration
HUH?
KYORO (GLANCE)
KYORO
MELISSA?
WHAT DO I DO?
WE GOT SEPA-RATED!
HEY, YOU!

HA (GASP)
IT'S THE GIRLS WHO BAD-MOUTHED MELISSA!
HOW DID YOU PASS...
...WHILE WE FAILED AND GOT KICKED OUT!?
HISO (WHISPER)
MELISSA COZIED UP TO THE TEACHER.
MU (SNAP)
HISO
UH-HUH. THAT SURE SOUNDS LIKE HER.

MELISSA WOULDN'T DO THAT!
HEH!
YEAH RIGHT.
BESIDES, YOU...
...ARE TOO USELESS TO DO ANYTHING.
......
GU (GULP)
HEY! STOP THAT!!
ZA (ZSH)
MELIS-SA!?
PAA (GLOW)

SHION!
I WAS WRONG!
HM PH!
FOR SHAME, TAKING OUT YOUR ANGER ON HER.
A ROTTEN HEART DISGRACES A WITCH'S DIGNITY.
YOU'RE ONE TO TALK.
YOU GO INTO HYSTERICS EVERY TIME YOU LOSE TO MELISSA.
BUCHI' (SNAP)
LEHM! FINISH THEM OFF!
DO (BLAM)
GYAAA (SHRIEK)
......

*SEE PAGE 67.

TH-THANK YOU.
PUI (SNUB)
I DIDN'T DO IT FOR YOUR SAKE.
SHE WISHES TO APOLOGIZE BECAUSE SHE BEHAVED SIMILARLY.
BE QUIET!
AND YOU, STAND UP FOR YOURSELF A LITTLE!
BUT THEY'RE RIGHT ...
I KNOW BETTER THAN ANYONE...
...THAT I'M A BURDEN TO MELISSA...
IF THAT'S HOW IT IS...
...WHY NOT QUIT BEING HER PARTNER?

I'M SURE YOU DON'T WANT TO BRING MELISSA DOWN...

...SO BREAK UP WITH HER.

IT'S TRUE THAT I'M INEXPERIENCED...

...BUT...

...I WON'T DO THAT.

GYU CCLENCH

84

...I WANT TO BECOME...

...THE ABSOLUTE BEST PARTNER FOR MELISSA!

TANYA!

THERE YOU ARE!

WELL, I'LL BE WATCHING.

...HMM.

MELISSA ...
YOU WANDERED OFF AGAIN.
MELISSA ...
...I'M GOING TO WORK HARD AND DO MY BEST HERE!
WHERE DID THAT COME FROM?
HEE HEE.
UGH! SHE'S THE WORST!
YOU TWO—
YOU'RE GOING TO LIKE WHAT I HAVE TO SAY.

The Witches' Ocean
TODAY IS AN EXTRA-CURRICULAR LESSON!
SEARCH FOR THE PEARLS WE USE IN OUR WEDDING ATTIRE...
...AND DEEPEN YOUR BOND WITH YOUR PARTNER.
...WAIT, WHY ARE THEY HERE!? THEY GOT EXPELLED LAST WEEK!
W—
WE WERE GIVEN A SPECIAL EXEMP-TION...
RIGHT...
...BECAUSE SHE REC-OGNIZED OUR TRUE POWER.
WE HAVE A DIFFERENT ASSIGN-MENT, SO...
OH HO HO HO!
...GOOD LUCK WITH THAT.

MUKIII (ROAR)
WHAT'S WRONG, MELISSA?
GIKU (JOLT)
N-NOTHING!
I'M A GOOD SWIMMER ...
...SO I'LL ACTUALLY BE USEFUL THIS TIME!
R-REALLY? I'M COUNTING ON YOU, THEN.
...HOW SHOULD I HANDLE THIS?
THE THING IS...
...I CAN'T SWIM.

I'VE SOMEHOW HIDDEN IT FROM TANYA SO FAR, BUT...
WILL YOU BE OKAY IN THE OCEAN?
I'M WATERPROOF.
...IT'S NOT REALLY POSSIBLE IN FRONT OF A CROWD.
I'LL TELL HER TO KEEP IT BE-TWEEN US...
TANYA, THE TRUTH IS—
MELISSA SWIM-MING...
I'M SURE YOU LOOK AS BEAUTIFUL AS A MERMAID!
UTTORI (SWOON)
URK!
IT'S GETTING HARDER TO ADMIT.
OH MY. A MER-MAID?
THAT'D BE A SIGHT TO SEE.
PFFT! HEH HEH!
GRRRR!
THAT WOMAN... SHE KNOWS!
ONLY ONE THING I CAN DO NOW...!!
LET'S GO, TANYA.

WATER PROTECTION SPELL—
ZAAA (FWOOSH)
MAXIMUM OUTPUT!!
I CAN USE WATER PROTECTION SPELLS LIKE THIS.
YOU'RE AMAZING, MELISSA! YOU REALLY CAN DO ANYTHING!
CHIKU (STAB)
W-WELL, KIND OF...

RADIATING MAGIC IS HONESTLY TOUGH...
...BUT NOW THAT WE'RE ALL THE WAY DOWN HERE, I HAVE NO CHOICE.
IT'S THEM!
LET'S GO, JUST LIKE WE PLANNED.
I WANT YOU TWO TO HELP ME UP THE ANTE OF THIS NEXT ASSIGNMENT.

GABU (BITE)
BACHIN (BURST)
!?

......!
BO
GOBO (GURGLE)
AM I... GOING TO DIE?
IF I'D KNOWN IT WOULD COME TO THIS...
...I'D HAVE BEEN MORE HONEST...

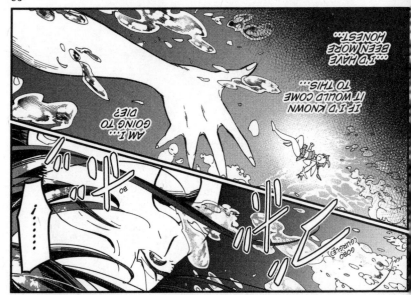

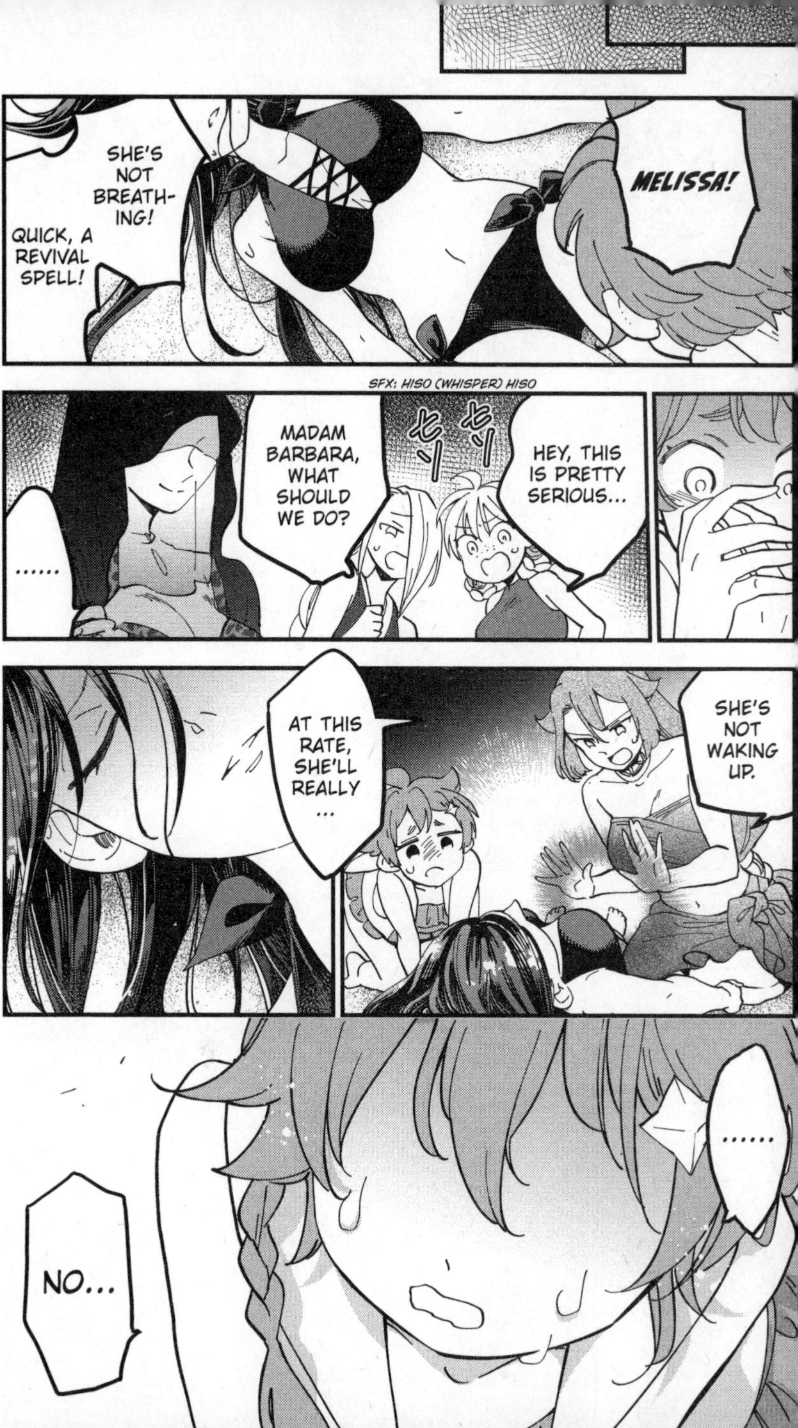
MELISSA!
SHE'S NOT BREATHING!
QUICK, A REVIVAL SPELL!
SFX: HISO (WHISPER) HISO
HEY, THIS IS PRETTY SERIOUS...
MADAM BARBARA, WHAT SHOULD WE DO?
......
SHE'S NOT WAKING UP.
AT THIS RATE, SHE'LL REALLY ...
......
NO...

COME BACK...MELISSA!!

PAAAAA
(GLOW)

!?
THAT'S A TIME REVERSAL SPELL.

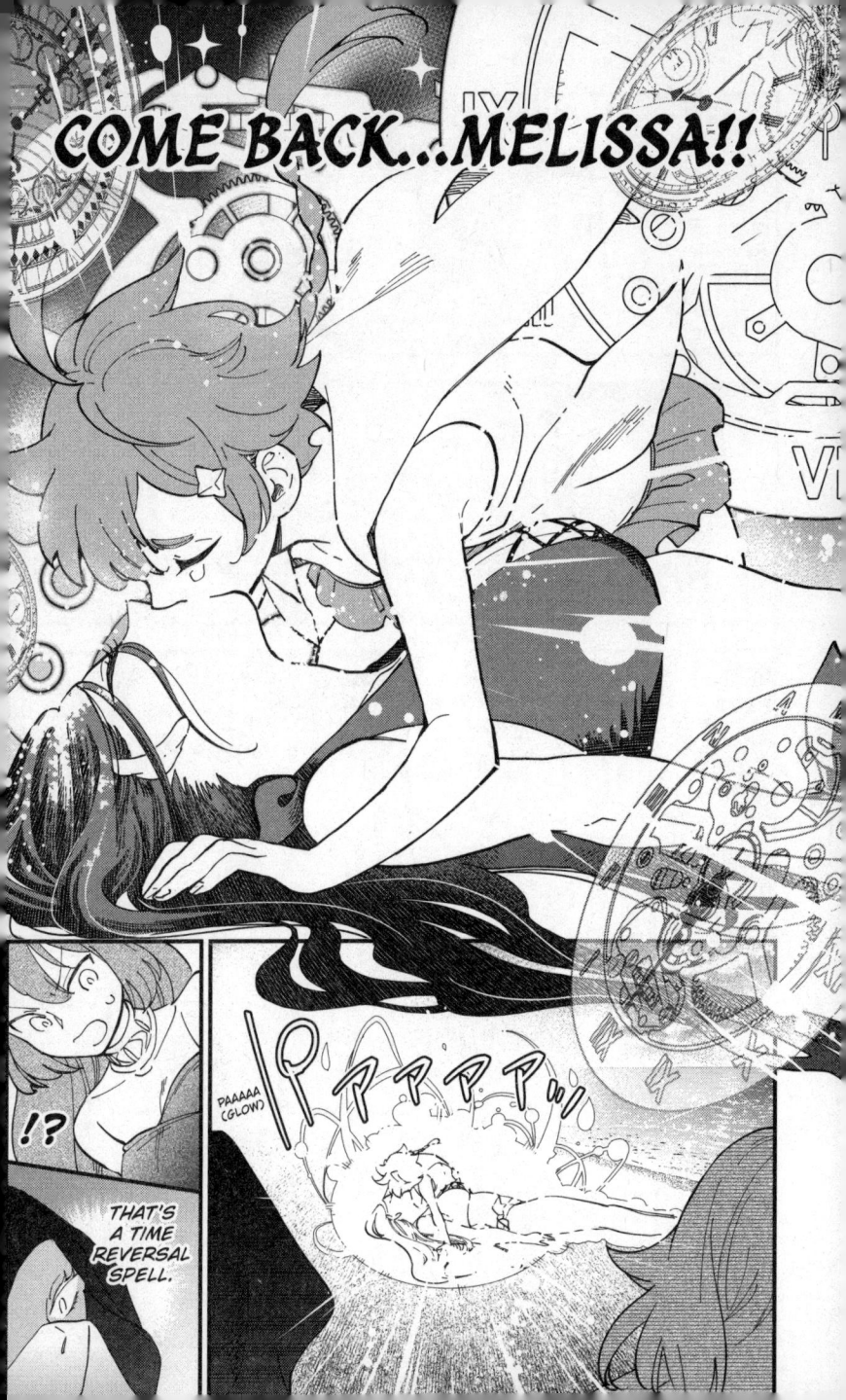

......

WA (CHEER)

SHE'S CON-SCIOUS AGAIN!

MELIS-SA!

TANYA?

I—I DON'T KNOW WHAT I'D DO IF YOU'D DIED...

I...I—

BURU (TREMBLE)

BURU

I'M SO SORRY FOR SCARING YOU.

I SHOULD HAVE TOLD YOU I CAN'T SWIM.

URK...
I'M SO GLAD...
WAAAAAH!
わあ
ああっ
I'M SO GLAAAAD!
AAAAH!
あ
ああ～ん
...MELISSA...
...APOLOGIZED FOR ONCE!?
THEY OVERCAME THE ACCIDENT...
...AND THEIR BOND GREW EVEN STRONGER.

THIS IS IT!
ZOKU
THIS IS WHAT I WANTED TO SEE! ♡
THE CARDS WERE RIGHT!
ZOKU (SHIVER)
KYAAAA (SQUEAL)
PERHAPS WE WENT A LITTLE TOO FAR...
MADAM BAR-BARA ...
ARE YOU KIDDING?

THE TRUE TEST OF LOVE...
...IS YET TO COME. ♥

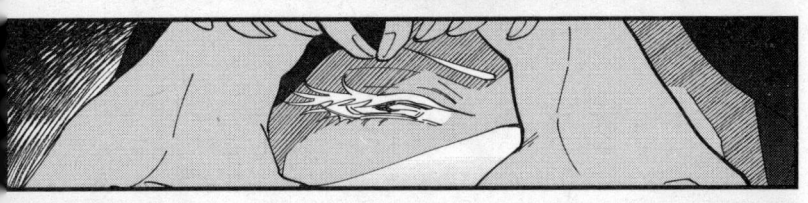

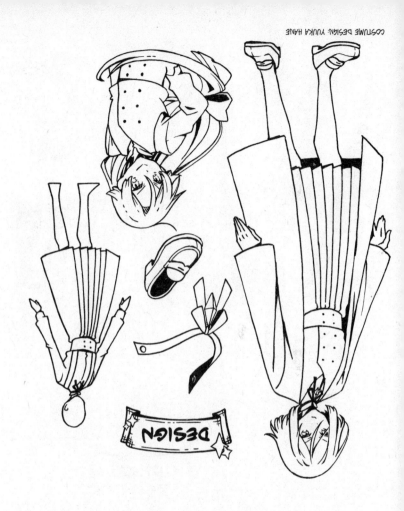

COSTUME DESIGN: YUUKA HANE

DESIGN

DESIGN
COSTUME DESIGN: YUUKA HANE

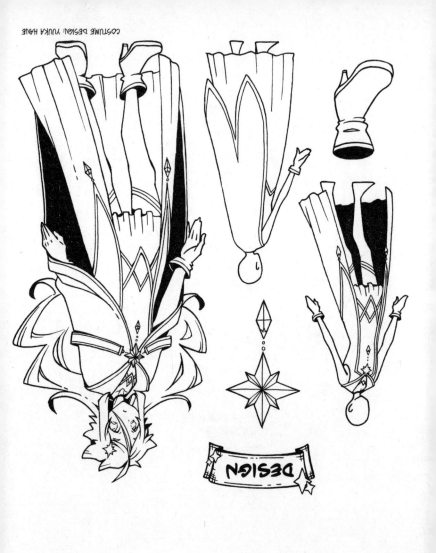

A WITCHES' DUEL—
TWO COUPLES, EACH JOINED IN A WITCHES' MARRIAGE, INCREASE THEIR RESPECTIVE BONDS AND MAGICAL POWER THROUGH COMBAT.
The Witch's Awakening
OKAY! NOW THEN...
...TODAY, I'LL HAVE YOU DUEL IN PAIRS.
I MAY BE IN A TEAM THIS TIME, BUT I'VE NEVER LOST A MAGIC SHOWDOWN.
I COULDN'T ASK FOR BETTER.
SINCE THERE ARE SO MANY OF YOU...
PACHIN (SNAP)
...WE'LL START WITH A QUALIFYING ROUND!

BASAA (FLAP)
A PHOENIX !?
ENDURE THE PHOENIX'S FLAMES FOR **TEN MINUTES**—
THAT IS THE QUALIFYING CHALLENGE.
YOU CAN USE ANY MEANS NECESSARY, SO WORK WITH YOUR PARTNER TO PROTECT YOURSELVES.
WITHSTAND TEN WHOLE MINUTES OF THAT HELLFIRE...?
ZAWA
ZAWA (MURMUR)
NO WAY! WE'LL BE ROASTED IN AN INSTANT.
OH DEAR! EVERYONE'S FRIGHTENED...
ZAWA
ZAWA

IF IT WERE ME, I COULD DO IT **ALL BY MYSELF**.
MU (SNAP)
BOSO (MUTTER)
I CAN DO THIS ALONE TOO.
ARE YOU SUUURE? NO NEED TO PUSH YOURSELF...
OH MY!
THIS WILL BE A BREEZE. I DON'T EVEN REQUIRE TANYA.
MELISSA !?
I'LL HELP YOU.
NO NEED. WATCH THIS.
POWA (FLOAT)
GO GO GO (RUMBLE)

GOOOO (ROOOOAR)
WHAT POWER!
JUUUU (SIZZLE)
THIS IS... PRETTY TOUGH.
I CAN—
I TOLD YOU, I'M FINE!

IT'S TOO LATE NOW TO ADMIT I CAN'T DO IT!
I WILL DO THIS MYSELF ...!
ジュウウウッ
JUUU
...!
ごくっ
GU (GULP)
YOU DON'T HAVE TO GO IT ALONE!

I MAY NOT HAVE MUCH EX-PERIENCE, BUT...
...I...
...AM YOUR PARTNER.
PLEASE ...
...RELY ON ME A LITTLE !!
...YOU'RE RIGHT.
THIS IS NO TIME TO LET MY STUBBORN-NESS GET OUT OF HAND.

PLEASE HELP ME...
...TANYA!
KUWA (ROAR)

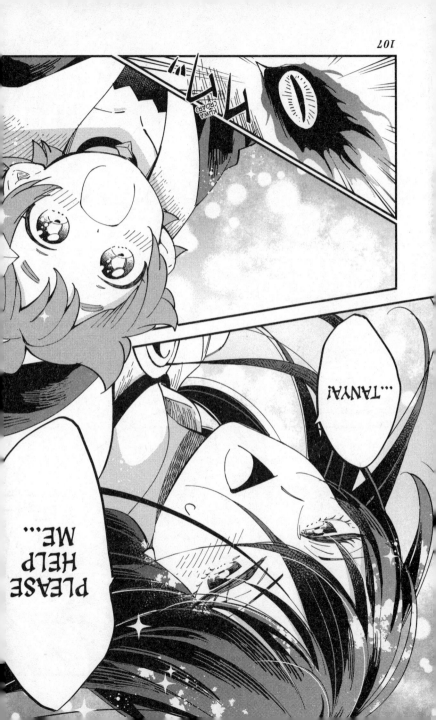

GOOO (FOOM)
!!
BA (FWIP)
MELISSA!!
KA (BOOM)

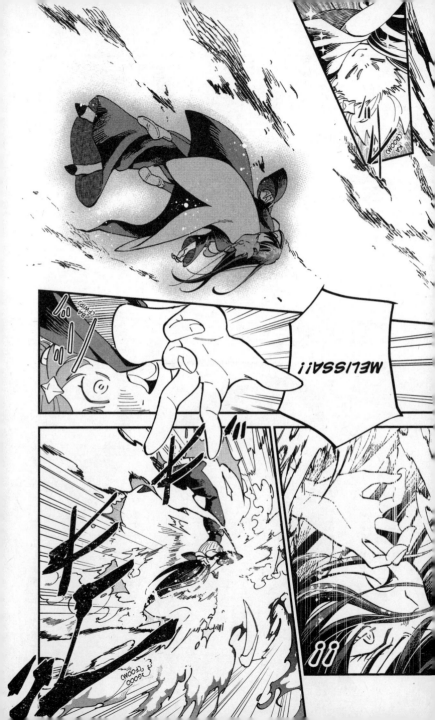

PAAAA
(GLOW)

THEY'RE
POURING
OUT LIKE
THEY'RE
IN FAST-
FORWARD
...

THE
FLAMES!

!? WHAT'S
THIS
...?

IT
STOPPED
...?

......

PUSU
(SPLUTTER)

PUSU

YOU ACCELERATED TIME FOR THE PHOENIX.
THAT'S A SUPER-RARE SPELL!
I KNEW IT.
YOU QUALIFY!
DAKI (HUG)
WE DID IT, MELISSA!
THAT WAS THE SAME SPELL AS BACK THEN...
DON'T TELL ME...
...TANYA'S POWER IS AWAK-ENING!?
NIYARI (SMIRK)

NIKO (SMILE)
NIKO
I DID SOME MAGIC TOO...
...AND IT WAS A SUPER-RARE TIME SPELL!
IF I KEEP UP THE GOOD WORK, I'LL CATCH UP TO YOU IN—
LIKE A POWER COUPLE.
SFX: GU (CLENCH)
YOU WON'T GET TO MY LEVEL THAT EASILY.
BOSO (MUTTER)
The Witches' Contest
MELISSA?
TSUKA
TSUKA (THUD)
BREAK TIME UNTIL THE MAIN FIGHTS!

MELISSA...
MAYBE SHE'S TIRED FROM USING TOO MUCH MAGIC...
WHAT CAN I DO...?
DID YOU HEAR? THE SCHOOL'S TRAVELING STORE SELLS MAGICAL YAKISOBA BUNS.
RUMOR HAS IT THAT EATING ONE INSTANTLY RECOVERS YOUR POWER.
REALLY? NO WAY!
THAT'S IT!!
AGNI'S TRAVELING STORE
WAI
WAI (GAB)
IT SELLS LIKE HOT-CAKES!
BUT I HAVE TO GET ONE.
HELLO, YOUNG MISS. YOU'RE IN LUCK.
THIS IS THE LAST ONE.
!

THANK GOODNESS—
NYU (REACH)
POWER-RECOVERING MAGICAL YAKISOBA BUN

AH.

LEHM.
TANYA.
BACHI (CRACKLE)
BACHI
I CANNOT RELINQUISH THE MAGICAL YAKISOBA BUN.

MADAM SHION'S ORDERS ARE ABSOLUTE.
GO BUY IT, LEHM.
W-WELL, I NEED IT FOR MELISSA!
...IT APPEARS ...
OH-HO-HO, THIS IS GETTING INTERESTING!
...THAT NEITHER OF US CAN BUDGE AN INCH.
I WILL NOT HOLD BACK.
GASHAN (CRACK)
GOKU (GULP)
A CONTEST !!

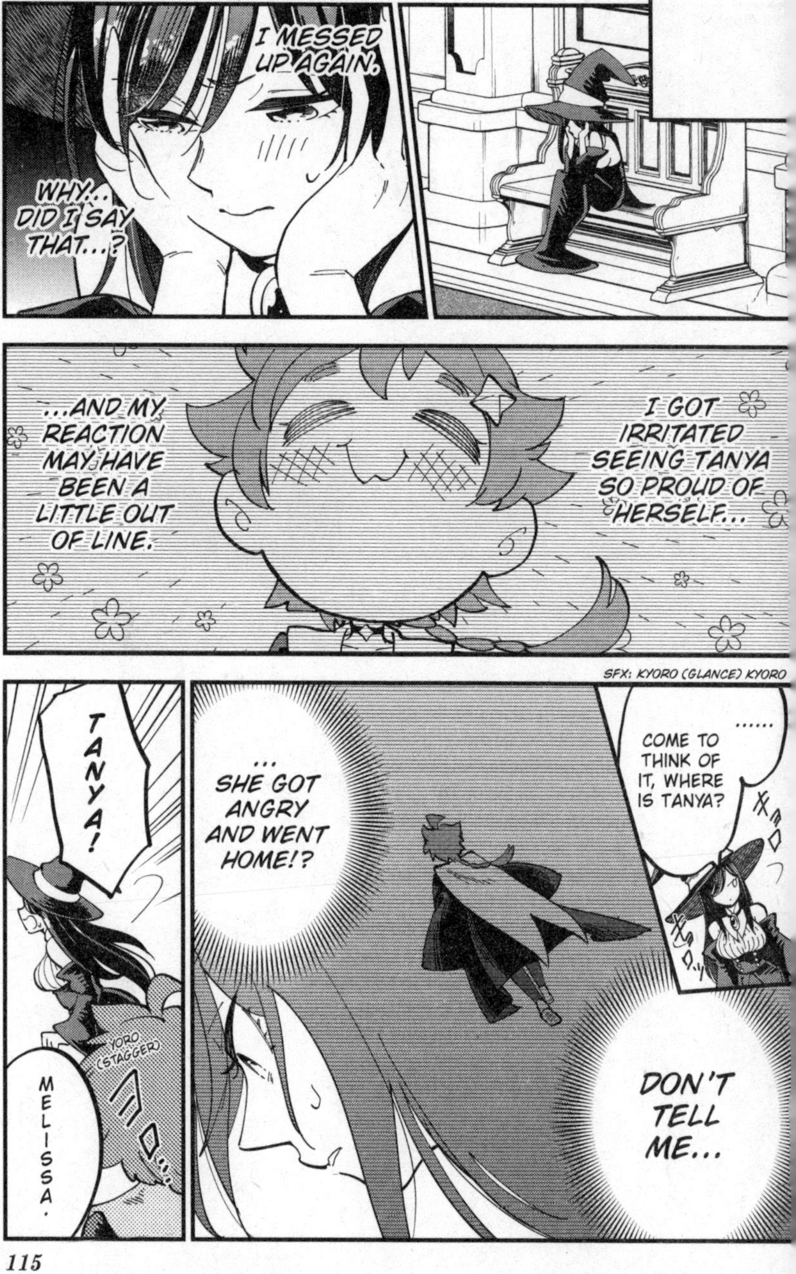
I MESSED UP AGAIN.
WHY... DID I SAY THAT...?
I GOT IRRITATED SEEING TANYA SO PROUD OF HERSELF...
...AND MY REACTION MAY HAVE BEEN A LITTLE OUT OF LINE.
SFX: KYORO (GLANCE) KYORO
......
COME TO THINK OF IT, WHERE IS TANYA?
... SHE GOT ANGRY AND WENT HOME!?
DON'T TELL ME...
TANYA!
YORO (STAGGER)
MELISSA.

ボロッ
BORO (TATTERED)
I WANTED TO CHEER YOU UP.
I... TRIED MY BEST, BUT...
SOB
...I LOST AT ROCK PAPER SCISSORS ...
WINNER
NEW PRODUCT
KASA (RUSTLE)
...AND THIS WAS ALL I COULD BUY...
SNIFFLE
FROG BUN
......

SU (SHF)
YOU WENT THROUGH ALL THAT TROUBLE? I'LL TAKE IT, THEN.
I'M ALWAYS ONLY THINKING OF MYSELF...
...BUT YOU PUT ME FIRST, DON'T YOU?

THANK YOU FOR EVERY-THING ...
... TANYA.
HEH HEH ...
NOT A CARE IN THE WORLD, HUH?
WE'RE NEXT ON THE BATTLE-FIELD ...
MUSHA
THERE I'LL SHOW THEM WHO'S BOSS!
MUSHA (MUNCH)

IT'S TIME FOR THE FINAL ROUND OF WITCHES' DUELS!
THE PAIRS FACING OFF ARE...
ZA (FWISH)
The Witch's Jealousy
I CAN'T BELIEVE YOU MADE IT THROUGH THE QUALI-FIERS.
YEAH, YEAH. TALK BIG WHILE YOU STILL CAN.
I KNOW WHAT SHION'S CAPABILI-TIES ARE.
THIS MATCH IS AS GOOD AS MINE.

THE FINAL ROUND IS A MAGIC BATTLE!
A SERIOUS SHOWDOWN WHERE ANY OFFENSIVE OR DEFENSIVE SPELL IS ALLOWED!
THE WITCH IN THE REAR IS THE SUPPORTER.
FROM THE MAGIC CIRCLE, YOU CAN SEND POWER TO THE FRONT WITCH!
THE WITCH IN THE FRONT IS THE ATTACKER.
THE MATCH ENDS WHEN THE OPPOSING PAIR IS UNABLE TO RECOVER OR FORFEITS!
BUT NO KILLING!
SUPPORT
ATTACK
THAT INCLUDES MY *TIME MAGIC*!
GOT IT! I'LL SUPPORT YOU WITH EVERYTHING I HAVE, MELISSA!
...I'LL LEAVE IT TO YOU...
OKAY!

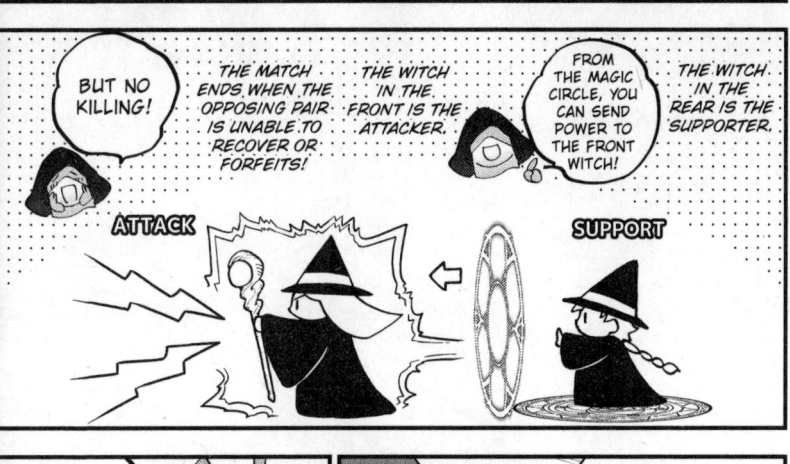

NOW...
...LET THE MATCH BEGIN!
SHA (SWISH)
GOOA (WHOOM)
DON (BOOM)

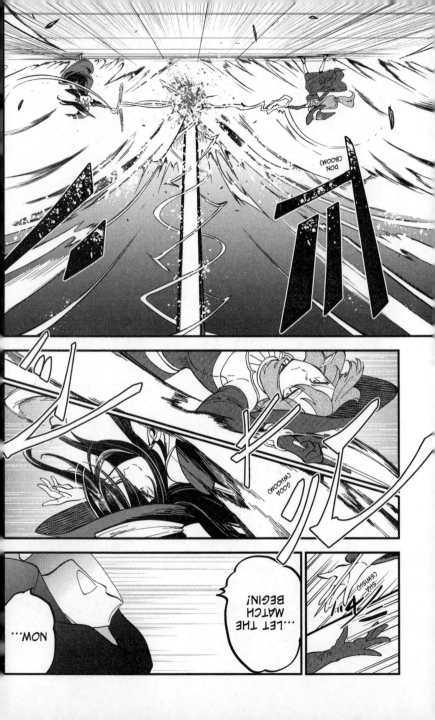

DODO (BANG)
THOSE TWO ARE AMAZING.
GOSA (WHOOSH)
DON (BOOM)
THEY'RE MORE OR LESS EVEN.
GUGU (STRAIN)
GUI (PUSH)
...HUH?
WAIT, DOESN'T IT LOOK LIKE ...

... MELISSA'S KINDA STRUGGLING?
HO HO HO!
WHAT'S WRONG, MELISSA?
LOOKS LIKE THE MOST YOU CAN DO IS DODGE!
GO (FWOOSH)
URK...
BACHIN (CRACK)
WE MAKE THE PERFECT COMBINATION ...
...UNLIKE YOU TWO.

TANYA! POWER, QUICKLY!
BUT...
...I'VE BEEN SENDING YOU POWER THIS WHOLE TIME...
WHY ...!?
THIS WAS TOO MUCH FOR TANYA AFTER ALL.
IF I WERE ON MY OWN—
YOU'RE WIDE OPEN!
DO (BOOM)
EEK! ☆

CLOSE CALL!
OOOH!
SO MUCH POWER... FROM SHION?
THIS MUST BE SOME KIND OF TRICK!
NOT AT ALL!
BOSO (MUTTER)
THIS TIME.
AS THE CIRCLE PUMPS MAGIC INTO THE WITCH IN FRONT...
...IT CAN EXTRACT MORE POWER THE STRONGER THE PAIR'S BOND IS.
SO WHY CAN'T WE DO THAT!?
OUR BOND IS MORE THAN—
...ALLOW ME TO EXPLAIN.
IT'S...

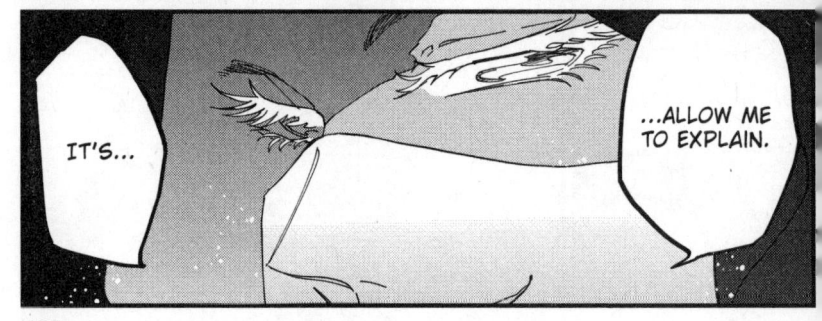

...ALL YOUR FAULT.
WHA...?
THE THING ABOUT A WITCHES' MARRIAGE ...
...IS THAT YOUR POWER INCREASES THROUGH MUTUAL ACCEPTANCE AND TRUST.
BUT YOU'RE NOT ACCEPTING LITTLE TANYA'S GROWTH.
YOU'RE JEALOUS!
THAT'S WHY...
...YOU CAN'T RECEIVE TANYA'S POWER. ♡

NO WAY... SOMEWHERE IN MY HEART...
...I STILL CAN'T ACCEPT...
...TANYA'S GROWTH!?
!?
MELISSA! IN FRONT OF YOU!
!!

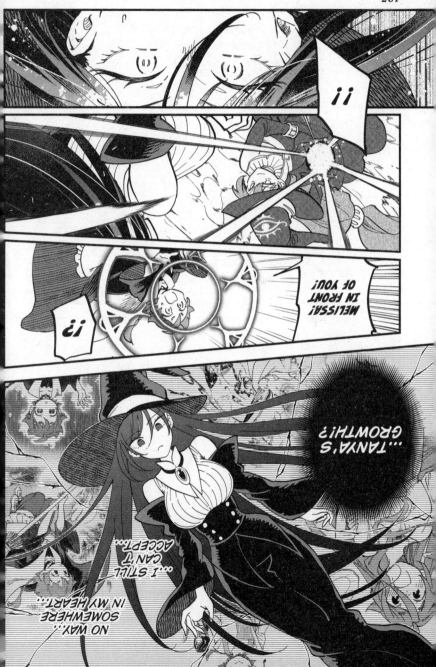

DON (BOOM)
...M...
MELISSA!!

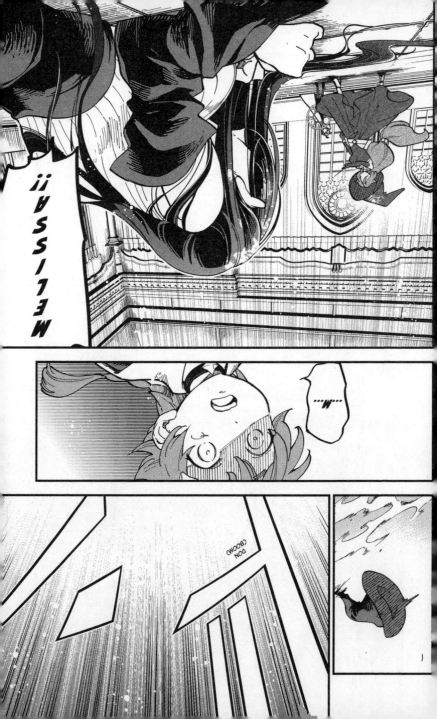

MELISSA!!

SO STUB-BORN.

AS IF...!

A CRITICAL HIT.

ORO ORO ORO (FRET)

THAT'S IT!

GIVE UP ALREADY.

129

IF I HEAL YOUR INJURIES BY TURNING BACK TIME—
PAA (GLOW)
!
STOP IT!
BIKU (JOLT)
OH, HOW RUDE! EVEN THOUGH YOUR PARTNER ...
...IS KINDLY TRYING TO SAVE YOU!
WHY, HMM ?
......
YOU DON'T WANT IT, DO YOU?
BECAUSE YOU'RE *JEALOUS* OF LITTLE TANYA'S ABILITY.
WHA ...?
KAAA (BLUSH)

THERE'S NO WAY THAT'S TRUE!
COMPARED TO ME, MELISSA IS...
...AN AMAZING WITCH WHO CAN DO ANYTHING!
...DID YOU HEAR THAT...
HEE HEE! ♪
...MELISSA THE AMAZING WITCH? ♪
......

IT'S—

...HUH?

IT'S NOT TRUE, RIGHT?

......

......

B-BUT HOW CAN AN INCREDIBLE PERSON LIKE YOU...

...BE JEALOUS OF SOMEONE LIKE ME...?

SA GURU

......

I...JUST WANTED TO BE USEFUL TO YOU...
...SO I WORKED HARD...
BUT INSTEAD...
...I ENDED UP CAUSING YOU PAIN...
NO...
I... DIDN'T MEAN TO...
DON'T SAY THAT!!

I ADMIT IT— SOME-WHERE DEEP INSIDE...
...MAYBE I WAS J- JEALOUS ...
BA (LIFT)
BUT ...!
TANYA'S WORKED SO HARD.
I ALWAYS ...
THAT'S RIGHT. I ALWAYS ...
... PLEASE ...
...BELIEVE THIS TOO—

I ALWAYS WISH FOR YOUR GROWTH, TANYA.

I TRULY DO.

SO LEND ME YOUR POWER...

...ONE MORE TIME.

HOW LONG ARE YOU GONNA MAKE ME WAIT!?
LET'S END THIS HERE.
LEHM, MAXIMUM POWER!
BA (FWIP)
GOOO (ROAR)
BYUN (WHOOSH)
BASHI (CRACK)
A DEFEN-SIVE SPELL !?
WHERE DID THAT STRENGTH COME FROM?

PAAAAA (GLOW)
I SEE.
YOU TURNED BACK TIME AND RECOV-ERED!
THANK YOU, TANYA.
NOW WE'LL SHOW HER OUR MAGIC.
OKAY!

パァァッ
PAAA (GLOW)
EEEEEEEEK!!
シュルルル
SHURURU (SHRINK)

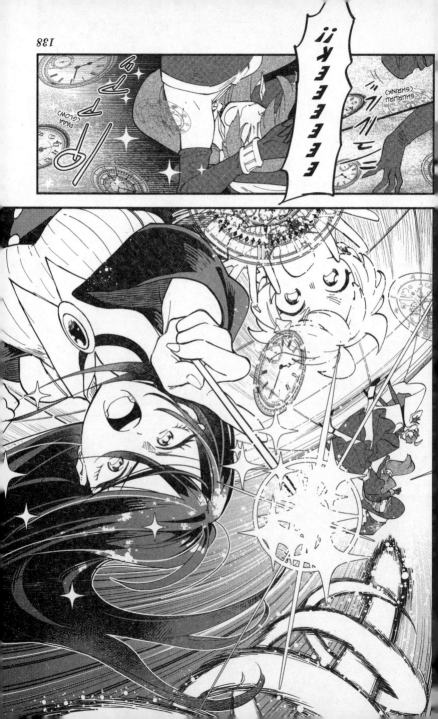

シュワワァー
SHUWAWAAA (FSSHHH)
WHAT'S GOING ON!?
TIME HAS BEEN REVERSED.
ワァァ
WAAA (CHEER)
THE WINNERS ARE...
...MELISSA AND TANYA!!
TANYA.
I MIGHT NOT BE ABLE TO LIVE UP TO YOUR IDEALS...
...BUT IF WE CAN STILL BE TOGE-THER—
...NO. I'M BEING SELFISH.
NEVER MIND.
......

TO BE HONEST ...
...I WAS A LITTLE SHOCKED.
SFX: GUSA (STAB)
BUT MORE THAN ANY-THING ...
...BY OPENING UP TO ME ABOUT YOUR WEAKNESS...
...YOU MADE ME VERY HAPPY!
HEY, QUIT BEING CLINGY.
KIIII (SCREECH)

DESIGN

COSTUME DESIGN: YUUKA HANE

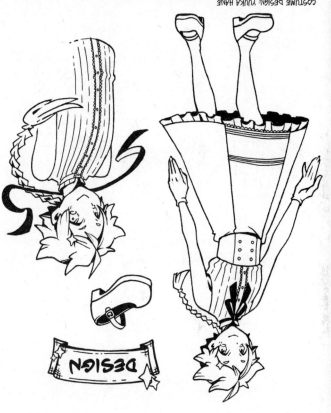

DESIGN

TA-DAA!!

NOOOOO!

LOVE マジョ

SWEATER: LOVE WITCH   COSTUME DESIGN: YUUKA HANE

MELISSA! MELISSA!
WHAT DO YOU THINK? DOES IT SUIT ME?
DOGYAAAAN (BAM)
LOVE マジョ
Bonus: The Witch's Happiness

SWEATER: LOVE WITCH

OOOOOOOOOOOO OOOOOOOOOOOO
IT'S... HIDEOUS!
...... UHH...... HMM.

KURU (TURN)
WHY IS TANYA'S AESTHETIC... SO...
...UNIQUE, I WONDER?
NOT TO MENTION HER SENSE OF HUMOR...
HER FOOD PRESENTATIONS ARE FINE, BUT HER FASHION...
EITHER WAY, THAT SWEATER IS JUST TOO MUCH ...!
WH—
BA (FWIP)
KYURUUUN (TILT)
THE HONEST GAZE OF SOMEONE WITH NO DOUBTS ABOUT HER STYLE.

URK...
PIKO (BOING)
PIKO
IT'S SUPER-CUTE, RIGHT!?
GU (CLENCH)
WHAT DO I DO...? I HAVE TO MAKE HER GIVE IT UP.
OTHERWISE...
...I'LL BE STUCK WALKING AROUND WITH THAT!!
HEE! HEE!
PFFT!
LOVE マジョ
KYAAAAGH!
きゃんっ
T-TANYA, WHY DON'T WE GET A COFFEE FIRST?
BUT THE SWEATER MIGHT NOT BE HERE WHEN WE COME BACK.
GYU (SQUEEZE)
ぎゅっ
NO ONE'S GONNA Buy THIS!!

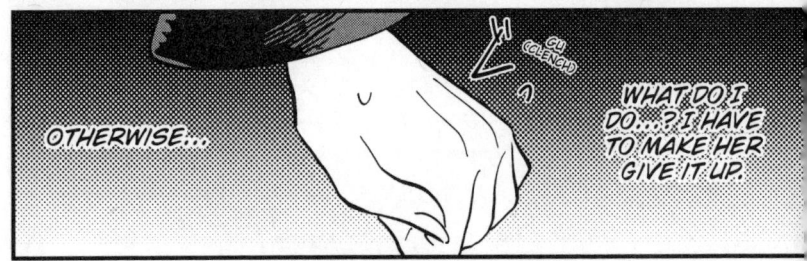

I NEED ANOTHER PLAN......
は
HA (GASP)
TANYA!
I'LL PICK OUT SOME CLOTHES FOR YOU!
WHAT!?
LOVE
ONCE SHE WITNESSES MY FASHION SENSE...
...WE SHOULD BE ABLE TO RETRAIN HERS.
YAY!
FIRST, TRY THIS!
LOVE

NATURALLY.
I'M
PERFECT.

...THIS IS
GREAT!!

NEXT, HOW ABOUT THIS OUTFIT?
AH... BUT THIS OTHER ONE MIGHT LOOK BETTER ON YOU...
HMMM...
......
HEE HEE.

I DIDN'T KNOW THAT CLOTHES SHOPPING WITH SOMEONE YOU LOVE...
...WOULD BE THIS MUCH FUN.
R- RIGHT...
KYUN (THROB)
IT'S NOT BAD ONCE IN A WHILE.
SO...

...IN RETURN...
...I'LL PICK OUT SOME CLOTHES FOR YOU!!!!!!!
HOW ABOUT MATCHING OUTFITS!?
DOGYAAAAN (BAM)
AAAAAAAGH!!
HAPPY Ending
LOVE
LOVE
SWEATERS: LOVE WITCH

MELISSA!
PLEASE TEACH ME SOME SPELLS!
Bonus: The Witch's Dream
THAT ONE AND THIS ONE AND THAT ONE...
TEACH ME ALL OF THEM!
I'VE GOTTEN SO GOOD AT MAGIC!
IN FACT, I'M EVEN BETTER THAN YOU NOW, MELISSA!
HUH?

PAAAAA (GLOW)

I HAVE
NOTHING
MORE TO
LEARN
FROM YOU.

......!?

NO!
GOODBYE, MELISSA.
TANYA, WAIT!!
GABA (FWAP)
HAA (PANT)
HAA
THIS DREAM AGAIN...
TANYA SURPASSING ME AND GOING AWAY...
THAT'S JUST...

FWOO...
WHAT'S WRONG?
...IT'S NOTHING.
I WAS TOO ANXIOUS TO SLEEP.
...IT'S TRUE THAT TANYA IS GROWING, BUT...
UN
...HER LEAVING ME?
UN (NOD)
THERE'S NO WAY.
OH, YEAH.

MELISSA!
PLEASE TEACH ME SOME SPELLS!
GIKU (SHOCK)
THAT ONE AND THIS ONE AND THAT ONE...
IT'S THE SAME AS IN MY DREAM!?
GYU (GRIP)
DOES THAT MEAN...

...SHE'S GOING TO LEAVE...
...LIKE SHE DID IN THE DREAM!?
ギュ
GU (CLENCH)
...BUT...
...I DECIDED THAT I WOULD...
...SUPPORT TANYA'S GROWTH!
FINE.
I'LL TEACH YOU ANYTHING YOU WANT.
THANK YOU!
HOLD ON! DON'T FORGET —

I WILL ALSO GROW...
...AS MUCH AS YOU DO!

?
NOTED.

THAT WAY, SHE SHOULDN'T LEAVE.

KOHON (COUGH)
...BY THE WAY...

......
GONYO (MUMBLE)
GONYO
HUH? WHAT IS IT?
... TONIGHT ...
SFX: PIYO (CHEEP)
P.YO!!
IF YOU WANT TO SLEEP TOGETHER ...
GONYO
...I WOULDN'T MIND.
SFX: CHIRA (GLANCE)
......
NIKOOO (SMILE)
ONLY IF YOU INSIST!
OKAY!

THE WITCHES' MARRIAGE
Staff Roll

EXECUTIVE PRODUCER/SUPERVISING EDITOR
TAKUJI HIROSE

DRAFT/STORYBOARD REVISION
GONTA AYAME

CHARACTER DRAWING
ENO

PROGRESS MANAGEMENT
TOGAWA

SHINO SHIMIZU	NAOTAKE	TETSU KIRIKI
TOSHINORI YANO	CHIYU	SHUN KASUGA
HINATA MIKAGE	HIROFUMI NEDA	AKIRA NOGAMI
YM KEI	YUUTO SAKASHITA	SHIORI AWAYA

KAMIN MORIWAKI	REIJIRO	MAO MORISHITA	RYUZAKI
YUUSHI HASHIMOTO	RITSU KUSAKA	RYUUKI FUKAHO	RYOJIRO IWAMA
AHUGAN SUGITA	MORIO	RIKKA HARUKI	KAWADA

COSTUME DESIGN
YUUKA HANE

DRAWING SUPPORT
MIKEY

PR
RIHO TAKASHIMA

SPECIAL THANKS
TATSUBON-SENSEI
TOKYO NAME TANK

COMIC NEWTYPE EDITORS
MATSUTANI, SASAKI, MATSUSAKA

BOOK DESIGN SAVA DESIGN

ALL OUR READERS

Twitter
@headline0003
PIXIV FAN BOX
headline.fanbox.cc

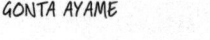

NOTE: STORYBOARDS (FIRST DRAFTS), BACKGROUNDS, AND FINISHING TOUCHES ARE ALL HANDLED BY THESE STAFF MEMBERS.

The Witches' Marriage

 2 studio HEADLINE

Translation: Eleanor Summers ✳ Lettering: Bianca Pistillo

MAJO NO KEKKON Vol. 2
©studio HEADLINE 2022
First published in Japan in 2022 by KADOKAWA CORPORATION, Tokyo.
English translation rights arranged with KADOKAWA CORPORATION, Tokyo,
through TUTTLE-MORI AGENCY, INC., Tokyo.

English translation © 2023 by Yen Press, LLC

Yen Press
150 West 30th Street, 19th Floor
New York, NY 10001

Visit us at yenpress.com
facebook.com/yenpress ✳ twitter.com/yenpress
yenpress.tumblr.com ✳ instagram.com/yenpress

First Yen Press Edition: December 2023
Edited by Yen Press Editorial: Ren Leon, Mark Gallucci
Designed by Yen Press Design: Liz Parlett

Yen Press is an imprint of Yen Press, LLC.
The Yen Press name and logo are trademarks of Yen Press, LLC.

Library of Congress Control Number: 2023938737

ISBNs: 978-1-9753-7023-7 (paperback)
978-1-9753-7024-4 (ebook)

1 3 5 7 9 10 8 6 4 2

WOR

Printed in the United States of America